FINISHING LINE PRESS
www.finishinglinepress.com

# Acrylic Angel of Fate

*poems by*

**Shirley McPhillips**

*Finishing Line Press*
Georgetown, Kentucky

# Acrylic Angel of Fate

ISBN 978-1-944899-07-3 First Edition


ACKNOWLEDGMENTS

Gratitude to the publications in which the following poems have previously appeared:

*Choice Literacy*: "Poemfields," "Life on the Edge," "Spring Villanelle," "The Porch in August," "Summer's a Gypsy," "Same Old Love Song: A Cento," "Invocation At the End of Summer," "Selfies of Autumn"
*Edison Literary Review*: "Same Old Love Song: A Cento"
*Journal of New Jersey Poets*: "Out of the Dust," "Single and Loving It?"

Editor: Christen Kincaid

Cover Art and Design: Ron Barrett

Author Photo: Eve Powell

Printed in the USA on acid-free paper.
Order online: www.finishinglinepress.com
also available on amazon.com

Author inquiries and mail orders:
Finishing Line Press
P. O. Box 1626
Georgetown, Kentucky 40324
U. S. A.

# Table of Contents

After Steepletop ........ 1

Same Old Love Song: A Cento ........ 2

Single and Loving It? ........ 3

Ruining the Image ........ 5

When the Pangaea split apart ........ 6

Ode to My Wig ........ 7

Music of Invention: An Interview ........ 8

Out of the Dust ........ 10

On the Wings of a Myth ........ 11

Messengers ........ 13

Poemfields ........ 14

Life on the Edge ........ 15

Spring Villanelle ........ 16

The Habit of Budding ........ 17

Birdhouse on the Old Outhouse ........ 18

The Porch in August ........ 19

Summer's a Gypsy ........ 21

Invocation at the End of Summer ........ 22

Selfies of Autumn ........ 23

Yesterday and Forever ........ 24

*For Sean, an enduring force*

*With special gratitude to Ron*

## After Steepletop

*(home of Edna St. Vincent Millay)*

I am composing like a goddess,
ever a hotbed of aesthetic

adventure, blinded
by steeplebush and lantana,

hungover like an apple bough—
ripe, rowdy, a blend of honey

and grit, steeped in the hot
jazz of the night.

The salty stride of illusion,
like a greyheaded ghost,

grieves in fresh torrents,
astonishing, fearless.

I am going to toss you my words—
if you catch them
they're yours.

## Same Old Love Song: A Cento

Like a honky tonk angel, notes
right on the downbeat, you hoax me

on wings of a dove in all the tender
places right through the night,

confusing love with longing
and thick with both. We get a little

crazy but never get caught.We
buy ice cream, see how far

we can drive before it melts,
strike matches just to watch them

burn. All this time my love,
honest as a robin, borderline blind,

we walk the line while the music
drops. My mama said there'd be

days like this when the heart
would crack just to let a little

light get in. She said I was making
a deal with the devil to bring

the angels home. Well, I've loved
like I should and lived like I shouldn't,

but if you're talking about a game
I can win, count me in. Otherwise,

it's hard to see past Friday night.

## Single and Loving It?

Most nights, Lila clutches her e-book,
strokes its faux pages, watches them curl
and turn over at her touch. A brave
kind of heat. Joanne

gave up her membership
in stayhitched.com. She scrolls
through people's travel photos online,
wonders, why haven't I walked
The Great Wall of China?

Isabelle hugs two secrets about Frank,
he still appears in her dreams
(they're erotic). And he was a lousy
table tennis player so she let him win.
But that was then. Marley

sips a single malt Scotch
and belts out hits with *Barbara Cook
Sings Sondheim:* I Wonder What
Became of Me. Send In The Clowns.

Annie thanks "the one" for a manic
outburst toward her at a party. She left
for the common good. She soaks
in her clawfoot tub and quotes Neruda:
*Full Woman, Fleshly Apple, Hot Moon.*

Maybe we like living alone Elizabeth muses,
because we're self-centered curmudgeons
who can't deal with others—

or because we'd rather search out
others instead of having them sit
in sweat pants on the couch.

## Ruining the Image

It isn't just that he lights the candle
at breakfast, the filigreed beeswax one

that sits between us on a coaster
of Klimt's portrait of *Emile Floge*;

the one that burns down fast and flickers out,
the last flame of regret revived.

A bit of wick drowns at the bottom
as smoke curls up through stagnant air.

It's not the staging he uses to lure me in
after he's backed away again. No, not that.

But the way he rubs the warm gel
with his thumb all over that woman's

wild curls, around her cherry-parted lips,
across her breasts heaved up
through a drape of jeweled mosaic.

## When the Pangaea split apart

molten rock spewed into the vulnerable spots
and hardened beneath the sun's blast.

Overlying rocks uplifted and eroded
to expose the palisades which stand today.

Two hundred million years later I straddle
a basalt boulder and gaze down at a floor

of forest castoffs—orphans of a long dry spell—
stick, acorn, curled oak. Topknots of hay
sprout from rocks, yesterday's sorrel and fern.

Late summer news leaves me parched.
How did this ball of igneous evil erupt
inside my breast—without the slightest tremor?

Some alien energy inside me writhes
beneath the faultline. I can feel it slip
and heave.

On the palisades, fine grains
of crystalline rock now glint
in the sharp light.

They call it
the *chill zone*.

## Ode to My Wig
*(AKA Hair-iette)*

Sweet disciple of deception,
taking a stand on my dressing table,
head held high among the picks,
the jewelry box, the eau de parfums.

At night, perched on your plastic pedestal,
you are my dis-connected diva, the faceless
heroine of my hirsute dreams. Your strands
stick out in honey-brushed abundance,

a crown of synthetic glory wafting
in perpetual stasis. Come morning, belle
of the bald pate, you defy my faithless
follicles, chemo-cowering in a vast

sebaceous-less wasteland. You give me
cover for my plot without a single
follicle to call your own.

Once, in my youth, when Miss Ada
arrived at worship in the sanctuary,
her topknot in fullblown fakery, we thought
she had traded her hat for a tea cozy

and sang derisive hymns with great joy.
But no such deviltry here. Though I
was tempted by the dark tresses
of the Russian virgin—

*you* are the acrylic angel who walks me
out the door with a straight face,
who keeps the strands of fate
swinging in my direction.

## Music of Invention: An interview

*You don't look*
*like your picture,*
*did you cut your hair?*

Comes from standing around
all day massaging the bones
of my writing hand, summoning
that old razzle dazzle.

*Do you write*
*at a proper desk*
*or on the backs*
*of napkins at Starbucks?*

In exile Victor Hugo wrote 100 lines
of poetry a day, standing up at a pulpit
looking out over the sea.
                                        The root
does not care where
its water comes from.

*Do you ever get ideas for poems*
*scribble them down in the night*
*then can't tell what they mean*
*in the morning?*

Ah, memory—the vapor trail
without which we are undone. My lines
seem to echo with the sound
of broken crockery.

*Are your poems about things that are true?*

A famous violinist
    *Have you won any medals?*
played a 1716 Stradivarius
for five hours
    *Any awards?*
in a Washington D. C.
subway at morning rush, and nobody
stopped to listen.

## Out of the Dust

Today I leave for the hills
before the fat air and sweet taunts
of the city stir the work wasps
into an unstoppable frenzy.

I head for a place where hawks
carve up clouds, where streams
tangle men in high-waisted boots.

I go to stake my claim, like a redwing
at the top of a northern pine, screaming
*this is my time*. I will sit still in clover,
let small sunsets of Indian Paintbrush

rise around my ankles, my hands hiding
in the folds of my dress. And when I grow
meek from painting hayfields and peaks

on a streak of mauve, I will laugh
into a gust of wind—Give me something
sacred to see I will cry, something bold
to bless. Give me something wild

to hold onto, fling me
screaming into blue flame, trick me
into a patch of passion, shake me dry
like a gourd until my seeds clamor
and crack again,

even if all that's left is dust.

## On the Wings of a Myth

Trail dust along the old canal
stirs up more stories

than I can outwalk,
but I am here, choking

in the backdraft between ruin
and the salt of desire, my knees

ground in the dirt of desertion.
Ghost barges still creak

through the stagnant waters
and my heart strains

along the towpath with the sweat
and pull of a cruel weight.

I am here, where grass
breathes up clover and stings

my wounded toes with dew,
where clouds tease the sky

at dusk and mountain gods
mumble the mysteries of the day.

I come here to heed the music
of memory—laid down

like some kind of rich sediment—
to remember why

when the sun flared too close
I kept on flying
and couldn't turn back.

## Messengers

There is a country where children
kneel at the graves of lost poets.

In the morning they come to the tomb
of Hafez and sing his poems back to him.

> *Where are the winds of spring and dawn?*
> *Where is the beat of the sun?*

In this way, before the arc of mind
ascends, they get associated with the heart—

the pull and tear as the outside
world stirs the linings of some

inside sky. Breathing in messages,
they outvoice his words
to the world:

> *So what toppled sweetness*
> *from the throne? So when*
> *did kindness die?*

## Poemfields

I have felt the hard knuckle
of winter, have gorged myself
with the intoxication of nothing

to be done. Among the circling
rituals of work and the pileup
of winter's wild edges, things

already named seem magically
strange. The deer grows grey
in winter light. The wind's pipes

haunt the air. Yet in the boundary
between myself and this landscape,
I am closer to what feels hidden.

Soon muddy roots will feed
the bloom. They will not let
their moment slip away,
unnoticed.

## Life on the Edge

The nest of my poem
is too loosely constructed

to hold much hope, all shreds
of thistledown and hay on the verge

of a ledge under the drainpipe,
sunblasted shortly after noon,

whipped by a race of rain
through scumbles of late clouds.

Day after day, a motherflurry
of wings, and the newborns, beaks
grub-woozy with expectation,

gape for a taste not altogether
alien. One bullies itself to the edge,
alive with a divine trembling.

How quickly its heart
beats in me.

## Spring Villanelle

Deep in the samadhi of the old pond
soft heavenly weather arrives, light
seeps into rock, enchanted by the eternal tide.

Peepers rise in a chime of bells
clear, connected by ancient notes
deep in the samadhi of the old pond.

Trees read the vernal signs, bear
the knowledge of arrival, their surge
seeps into rock, enchanted by the eternal tide.

The deer stalks through a fine mist
dark among the black trees, shadows
deep in the samadhi of the old pond.

A redwing's cry shatters time running
and standing, a tinge of rhyme
seeps into rock, enchanted by the eternal tide

Joy, behind the rise of happy tears
cracks the iron darkness of the heart
deep in the samadhi of the old pond
seeps into rock, enchanted by the eternal tide.

## The Habit of Budding

1

Weaned in its first year
a calf rubs its budding horns

against the fence to feel a heart
pulse back.

2

A tree cut down by nature's
wise ax will sprout again.

Though its root grows old
in the earth and its stump
dies in open ground,

at the scent of water
it will bud and put forth branches.

## Birdhouse on the Old Outhouse

Outside, where the sun
strong arms its way through

a twist of sumac and cracked stems,
a small house holds onto

a loose board, itself unsure
what the next wind will unhinge.

An artist might lay in a shadow
of indigo at the back for shape,

an anchor to make it stay
on the page, an illusion

of permanence. At the front,
a hole so small only a particular light

could kindle in that dark place,
could feel safe gazing out
at such a round world.

## The Porch in August

I stand on the stage
of morning, the meadow
still stained with moonlight,

trying to pick up the fragments
of a character I thought I knew
over this extended run.

The sky pushes back a curtain
of cloud to eye the day,
and I am sky.

Crows caucus down by the creek,
all squawk and wingflap,
and I am crow.

I am the redwing that rises
out of meadowgrass
into a surprise of sumac.

I am finch meditating
on fenceposts, facing east
through the milkweed.

I am cricket murmuring
in the zinnia bed, a slim
crust of song.

I am the jewelweed that lifts
a lantern for the hummingbird
who cues me my pale words.

Bees follow their bliss
into a wallow of sage,
and I am bliss.

I step out barefoot
into a bite of nettles
and shake loose

my hair. I am
an uncertain player.
I am air.

## Summer's a Gypsy

She takes the hand of Juno
and walks through a thin wash
of rain into light. Her toes loosen

the quickening earth. She stops
to weave the lush strands of her hair
with bittersweet and vine.

A strum of windharp and wave
invades her feet and the dark tones
of the Whip-poor-will's call

deepen in her bones. At the whine
of the cicadas, the mad click-click
of their tymbals, she pulls her bandana

tight around her head. Her bodice
shimmies with ribbons and bells;
she gathers up the bounty of her skirt—

a glaring clash of wing, leaf, star—
and vamps headlong into the struggle
between dog days and the divine.

Beguiled by the heat of her fandango,
we hold out our palms and bid her
tell us what she knows

of lifelines and longing
old as wildfire.

## Invocation at the End of Summer

I call on the spirit of summer's end,
of tangled roots and the earth's
mold. Give me your hum.

I call on things that thrive in byways—
snakeroot, aster, dock. The teasel
that pricks, the pod that slips away.

Give me light, charged with a flush
of quick shadows—the sun stretched
flat across the grass, sullen, satisfied.

Let me feast on the overripeness of things,
the spice of apple that dazzles wasps
and spins deer in drunken staggers
over the field. Give me your heat.

I call on things that sweeten and fall—
butternut, pippin, the fluttering hearts
of rosebud—the luscious drip of evening,

a shuddering of birds rising up
and settling, the last secrets of the katydid.

Let me put my head among the leaves.
Let me listen.

## Selfies of Autumn

*(for Barbara Caldwell)*

The day drips with the elixir
of autumn—a dark honey
of orange, a sadness of red,
the steadfastness of green.

A rainpool of birds slap
the summer's heat from their wings;
beaks strip their feathers as if
to neaten up for a brave new day.

In the garden, I pose with the ghosts
of spring peonies. I can still breathe
their ambrosia heavy as wine, still feel
their heads lean.

Along the woodpath, squirrels
tear and leap, leap and tear, delirious
with an onset of primal intuition.

Above them the bittersweet vine,
blood-burned, still wants to reach,
to wind.

A windburst stirs the leaves
to the gripping point. One golden
soul, all lightness and fluttering heart,
twists and soars.

But time just won't, I think,
allow for drift. I'll snap a picture
for eternity, I say. *You and me*
*against the starry cold.*

## Yesterday and Forever

Standing on the corner of 66th
and Broadway the first day of the new
year, you speak of the cracking
sound you hear when expectation

meets reality—the need to set down
that bag of fevered questions
before the bottom splits wide open.

The wind cuts corners and stings
our cheeks. I feel the vague sensation
of a heart brimming with old days—
our first new year in a winter wood:

Moss where we stroll shimmers
a mythic green. Under the wooden bridge,
the stream holds a mystery of murmurs
and shadows.

Leaves underfoot, at ease among
the scattered lightfall of a weakened sun,
have lost their crunch. The silence
has no name.

Our gloves safeguard a growing energy
that lingers when we touch. Our shy
mouths hunt for words. We listen
with all our might.

Seems like forever.
Seems like yesterday.

A classroom teacher for many years, **Shirley McPhillips** has also worked as a literacy staff developer, conference speaker, institute leader and writing consultant.

Her poems have found homes in journals such as *Edison Literary Review, Journal of New Jersey Poets, Sewanee Review, Frogpond, Poets Online*, and elsewhere.

She is Poet Laureate for *Choice Literacy* (choiceliteracy.com) and is a member of the Writers Council of the National Writing Project (http://www.nwp.org/cs/public/print/doc/about/writers_council.csp).

Shirley co-authored, with prize-winning poet and memoirist Nick Flynn, *A Note Slipped Under the Door: Teaching from Poems We Love* (Stenhouse Publishers, ME, 2000).

Her current book, *Poem Central: Word Journeys with Readers and Writers*, (Stenhouse Publishers, ME, 2014) introduces us to professional poets, artists, teachers and students—people of different ages and walks of life—all engaged in reading and making poems.

In addition to writing, Shirley paints watercolors, travels, sings sixteenth-century music and walks with nature. She believes in the power of poems to illuminate the ordinary—to nurture, inspire and stand alongside us for the journey.

www.ingramcontent.com/pod-product-compliance
Ingram Content Group UK Ltd.
Pitfield, Milton Keynes, MK11 3LW, UK
UKHW042011190726
13854UKWH00005B/2237